What People Are Saying

A Primer on Utopian Philosophy

The driving force behind Greenaway's exegesis of Ernst Bloch's work is the much-needed task of rediscovering hope — not in the form of naive optimism or passive wishful thinking, but in the struggle to find the seeds of utopia in everyday life, to see in the quotidian the "unbearable nearness of utopia."
Jonas Čeika, author of *How to Philosophize with a Hammer and Sickle*

Jon Greenaway shows us that the world is infinitely full of hope, and yes, for us too. Bloch is revealed to us as the romantic materialist who is only too ripe for a full-on revival for the Left today. A thinker who teaches us to embrace the rupture of utopia as the rupture hidden within all previous history, the Old Man with the Raised Fist still has much to teach us!
Adam C. Jones, *Acid Horizon*

Ernst Bloch has been a relatively minor figure within the intellectual history of the Left, until recently. As interest in his work grows, I can think of no better introduction to his work than this book — a super accessible and invigorating read!
Matt Colquhoun, author of *Narcissus in Bloom: An Alternative History of the Selfie*

An important intellectual history of hope's chief philosopher, Greenaway's book reanimates one of European Marxism's most elusive figures, with a clarity and urgency fitting of the challenges presented by Bloch's great utopian gamble. A welcome and necessary contribution from a rising voice on the Left.
Kyle Kern, historian & YouTuber

The philosophy of Ernst Bloch has shaped generations of Marxist philosophers, from Theodor Adorno and Gyorg Lukács to Fredric Jameson, but rarely is Bloch assessed on his own terms in the full range and depth of his thought. Jon Greenaway has managed to bring the fullness of Bloch's concepts into the urgent light of our present, from his theory of fascism, consciousness, revolution, class struggle, and religion to the nature of reality itself. Greenaway's ...*Introduction to the Work of Ernst Bloch* is an inspired and beautifully written introduction to the revolutionary thought of Ernst Bloch.
Daniel Tutt, author of *How to Read Like a Parasite: Why the Left Got High on Nietzsche*

"There is an infinite amount of hope in the universe," someone once said, "but not for us." And yet, in an age of economic crisis, ecological catastrophe, and social declension, hope can be nothing less than a revolutionary imperative; it is the name for our collective desire that life might be lived together and otherwise. What this book shows, with an erudition born of love and fury, is that hope might yet be the fire with which we blaze the path to utopia, incinerating this terrible universe along the way.
Mark Steven, author of *Class War: A Literary History*

A PRIMER ON UTOPIAN PHILOSOPHY

AN INTRODUCTION TO THE WORK OF ERNST BLOCH

Jon Greenaway

London, UK
Washington, DC, USA

CollectiveInk

First published by Zer0 Books, 2023
Zer0 Books is an imprint of Collective Ink Ltd.,
Unit 11, Shepperton House, 89 Shepperton Road, London, N1 3DF
office@collectiveinkbooks.com
www.collectiveinkbooks.com
www.zero-books.net

For distributor details and how to order please visit the 'Ordering' section
on our website.

Text copyright: Jon Greenaway 2023

Paperback ISBN: 978 1 80341 327 3
eBook ISBN: 978 1 80341 670 0

A CIP catalogue record for this book is available from the British Library.

Design credit(s): Lapiz Digital Services

UK: Printed and bound by CPI Group (UK) Ltd, Croydon, CR0 4YY
Printed in North America by CPI GPS partners

We operate a distinctive and ethical publishing philosophy in
all areas of our business, from our global network of authors to
production and worldwide distribution.

ACKNOWLEDGEMENTS

I would like to acknowledge the help of the entire team at Zer0 Books for their editorial guidance and Carl Neville for the kind invitation to write something on Bloch's work.

Without the work of a small number of Anglophone scholars, much of Bloch's work would have remained a closed book to me, so I must acknowledge the writing of Cat Moir, Peter Thompson, Wayne Hudson, Fredric Jameson, and Vincent Geoghegen as being profoundly illuminating in a whole variety of ways.

This book, like everything I write, is dedicated to Emma, without whom it would not exist.

CONTENTS

BEGINNING AT THE END: HOPE IN AN AGE OF DISASTER

How did we end up here?

On 4 November 2008 at Grant Park in Chicago, the president elect, Barack Obama, took to the stage and thanked his supporters after his historic win in the fight for the US presidency. 'This is our moment', said Obama. The iconic image of Obama's campaign, a stylised stencil drawing of Obama's face, had been designed by the American artist Shepard Fairey with one word emblazoned underneath: hope. The Obama campaign's rhetoric suggested a great coming together of all peoples, that if *we* tried hard enough and worked hard enough and believed then all our hopes could well be fulfilled. Of course, what that meant in practice was two terms of disappointment, of passively watching the political structures of American imperialism thrash along and the promised better things never really arriving.

In the wake of 2008, and in the wake of the Trump presidency, the COVID-19 pandemic, the series of crises of capitalism that have wracked much of the modern world and the ever-grinding news of exploitation and violence which sustains so much of our shared existence, hope cannot help but seem like a distant idea at best and, at worst, undeniable quietism in the face of disaster. To talk of Utopia means reckoning with the question Brecht asked in his poem "To Those Born Later": 'What kind of times are they, when/A talk about trees is almost a crime/Because it implies silence about so many horrors?' After all, the grand narratives of possibility have seen a seismic collapse over past decades, and you would be hard pressed to find many who speak of Utopia with a straight face anymore. Utopia has become a relic — a thought from a different age. For those on the left in particular, the temptation is always towards a cold-eyed assessment of how things are, and hope, with its soaring speeches and future looking speculation can all too often be an excuse for refusing to see the world as it truly is. In an era of climate catastrophe, look at the world burning in the fire of extractive capitalism and hope turns to ash.

Yet, at the same time, hope is necessary. As Tom Whyman points out in their book *Infinitely Full of Hope*, 'if reality as it presently exists appears to have nothing to offer you, then you may as well attempt to live in an alternative one: if you really have nothing to hope for, then by rejecting reality you'd have nothing to lose.' If the future is decided, if hope completely absents the stage then why bother with the idea of anything different? No hope, no future, and certainly no Utopia. What makes hope distinctive is the possibility of agency — the idea that we can *do something different.*

Perhaps it is best to turn away from hope. What that leaves us with are a couple of bleak choices. One, a passive optimism that simply wishes things could be different, or two, a nihilistic abandoning of the world, allowing it to get worse (of course, these two things can often go hand in hand). If the rhetoric and idea of hope and Utopia has often been used for the narrow and cynical purposes of political sloganeering, perhaps this is not grounds for discounting hope entirely. Perhaps the problem is not that hope is too easy — a way of dodging the hard questions of politics and philosophy — but that hope is far harder, more complex, and more ambitious than we would like to admit. Much of what passes for hope is maybe best understood as optimism, the sense that things will work out and our own involvement in the question of how really isn't all that important. To put this another way, who needs hope when the wonderful outcome that the optimist predicts is, in some way, just a given? If hope is to be taken seriously as a political necessity and philosophical idea then we cannot be satisfied with an easy notion of hope that rests upon a temporary political success, a subjective feeling of participation or all too brief moments of possibility. If hope is to be taken seriously, it requires not just a re-thinking of our politics but a complete reconstruction of philosophy from the ground up. Optimism is easy – it looks at this world, full of the great sea of human suffering and has the gall to be satisfied. Hope is *hard* and so to move past the platitudinous means a radical engagement with thought in all its forms.

The reason for this necessity is that if optimism is all too often concerned with the present, then hope is the discourse of the future. The optimist might think the future will be alright in the end but the forces which let them think that are already at work in the here and now. A common example might be how we admonish people for criticizing billionaires such as Jeff Bezos or Elon Musk because they are going to take us to Mars or save the world in the future. The optimist looks at the world as it is now and sees it slowly continuing into a future that will look ... pretty much the same as what we have now. In contrast, hope is not simply idle, but carries with it a sense of agential possibility. To hope for something is to see a relationship between the conditions of the present and the fulfillment of hope in the future. Confronted with the conditions of our present, there will be those who see hope as a kind of foolish self-deception at best and unforgivable stupidity at worst, but this is, I would argue, more a reflection of the limited ways in which we talk about hope generally, rather than a problem with hope as a philosophical and political category of thought. Hope is the philosophical counterpart to the political project of Utopianism — the jaw-dropping, incredulous idea that the world could move beyond the rapacious violence of capitalism. There is an astonishingly, staggeringly ambitious gamble at the core of hope, perhaps best expressed in the famous words of Rosa Luxemburg:

> Bourgeois society stands at the crossroads, either transition to socialism or regression into barbarism. Today, we face the choice exactly as Friedrich Engels foresaw it a generation ago: either the triumph of imperialism and the collapse of all civilization as in ancient Rome, depopulation, desolation, degeneration — a great cemetery. Or the victory of socialism.

We are now over a century further from the time those words were written, and it seems, in many ways, that the crossroads have been left in the distance. But even so, if the crisis has intensified then it is imperative to try and find new avenues of thought that might help us to move beyond it. As the philosopher Cat Moir puts it, '"Utopia or bust" may be a bold wager, but the insidious attrition of utopian desires in fear of the "or bust" alternative is... a much darker prospect'.

If we are to try and reconstitute hope as a philosophically and politically viable idea, then we need resources — tools that can be turned to the great challenge of bringing into being what is 'not yet'. For this, one of our greatest resources is the work of the philosopher, Communist, utopian, atheist theologian and writer, Ernst Bloch. Bloch's magnificent corpus stretches across the very end of the nineteenth and the beginning of the twentieth century, an audacious experiment in form and thought aimed at making hope into not just an idea, but an ontological and philosophical principle of existence itself. His work is little read in the Anglophone world due to the simple fact that much of it remains untranslated. Even when it has been translated, Bloch's style of writing — allusive, associative, complex, philosophically dense, and unabashedly literary — does not lend itself to ready exposition. It is philosophy written as literary modernism and so there are many versions of Bloch that have arisen over the years. For Fredric Jameson, Bloch is something of an allegorist, doing for Marxism what Medieval

Scholastic theology did for Christianity. For Jurgen Habermas, Bloch was a Marxist Schelling, a pre-critical poet whose writing was less philosophy and more prophecy. For the apparatchiks of the DDR (Deutsche Demokratische Republik), Bloch was a revisionist, a theologian who had wandered from the true path of socialism and who had to be blocked from teaching and publishing. For some of those in West Germany, when Bloch stayed on their side of the Berlin Wall, he was an apologist for Stalinism — a throwback to the naivety of socialism; a figure of fun at worst, and one of pleasant nostalgia at best.

Despite all these claims, each with its own degree of truth, his work has continued to draw people in, exemplifying a restless and relentless search for the potentiality of the future within the present. Rather than get caught up in trying to answer all the charges, to dispel the ghosts of all the different kinds of Ernst Bloch that exist in the pages of so many books, the aim of this short book is to treat Bloch primarily as a philosopher and his Utopian project entirely in keeping with a valuable tradition of thought. More exactly, Bloch's work is a certain kind of philosophical hermeneutics — an interpretation of the world that fundamentally alters how we think about all things.

Before proceeding too much further it's worth adding a couple of necessary caveats. Time and space mean that an exhaustive exegesis of Bloch's concepts is simply not possible. His work is recursive and often narrativistic with concepts being connected across distinct works. The meaning of ideas gets worked out in the course of Bloch's writing, deepening through association, allusion, and connection so that to read Bloch's work is not to follow a strict logical argument but to have the ideas emerge organically from the language in a way that is often deeper and more emotionally resonant than they would have done with a more straightforward structure. To try and give a traditional exegesis of Bloch's work would make this book of equal length as his own. (At the end of this book I've recommended some useful sources for those who want to follow the threads of Bloch's work a little further.) Those familiar with Bloch will no doubt take issue with some of my points as being too one-sided or too in-depth and so rather than mistake the map for the territory, I can only plead guilty to the charge of glossing things where I judge it necessary. Rather than a scholarly monograph on Bloch, this is a *primer.* The term is most commonly used in decorating — to prepare a wall for paint you use a primer. If you want to detonate a charge, it must be primed first. A primer is the very start of something; something that prepares the ground for you to do with as you will.

So, after a brief introduction to Ernst Bloch's life and intellectual context, this primer goes through his philosophy of history, covering some of Bloch's most important concepts such as non-synchronicity, latency and possibility, the objectively real-possible and the vital idea of the 'not yet'. From there we turn to the politics that this philosophy of history demands — a polyphonic dialectical Marxism that aims not at some static model of state Socialism, but at the place wherein all humanity could, as Bloch put it, walk upright, as if for the first time. To conclude, the primer finishes with Bloch's magnum opus, the beautiful, loquacious, occasionally challenging but never boring book *The Philosophy of Hope.* We are, in so many ways, at the end of hope; Obama's slogan now a punchline and a stand-in for a weary kind of political cynicism. In an era where political hope seems only to exist to be crushed, when the left has racked up a century of defeat and setback, shouldn't we give up all these notions? 'Don't mourn, organize', says the classic leftist imperative, but for all the frenetic activity how far have we gotten? But, as Bloch pointed out himself, Genesis comes at the end, not the beginning. Perhaps here, even now, there is the possibility of recuperating the philosophy of hope, of looking at the world and seeing not the gray deterministic malevolence of capitalist realism but something struggling to come into a fullness of being. Not just new modes of life, but new knowledge too. For as Bloch put it, philosophy will have conscience of tomorrow, commitment to the future, knowledge of hope, or it will have no more knowledge.

Ernst Bloch was born in the city of Ludwigshafen on July 8, 1885. Ludwigshafen was a new city of capitalism; industrial, polluted and often poor. Across the river lies Mannheim, famed even today for its eighteenth-century palace, its plaza with beautiful fountains and venerable university. This split between the worlds of bourgeois luxury and proletarian exploitations was something Bloch would write about in his early and autobiographical work *Spuren* (Traces) — underscoring the extent to which capitalistic class contradiction is something which we all live through, and which cannot help but shape our developing political sense of the world as it surely shaped Bloch's own. All the various sources for his early life tell us of a bookish, imaginative and undeniably intelligent young man, who presumably found schoolwork and traditional academia rather boring. He was precocious and was, by the time he was a teenager, writing his own original philosophy and corresponding with leading German intellectuals. As he would later put it, 'there is only Karl May [a famous German writer of adventure stories] and Hegel, everything in between is an impure mixture'. Yet despite all of this, he didn't have a glowing academic reputation. As his school report from 1904/5 argued: 'his achievements are so minimal that, considering the profound gaps in his knowledge, he will only be able to pass his final exams by the most strenuous application'.

Yet pass them he did, and he moved on to Munich and Wurzburg to study philosophy, falling in with the crowd around the fashionable academic Georg Simmel, known for his *Lebensphilosophie* (philosophy of life) that allowed for theorising on everything from metaphysics to romantic love. From there, Bloch moved around Berlin and made perhaps the most important connection of his early life, the Hungarian philosopher and literary critic, Georg Lukács. By 1911 he was already developing the first articulations of his own philosophical concepts, such as the 'not yet conscious' (more on that later). Lukács and Bloch quickly became inseparable, forming a close friendship and an intellectual partnership. Bloch was, in this early stage of his life, fascinated with German philosophy and culture, and found his relationship with Lukács was a way of synthesising this interest with political radicalism. Following the philosopher and expert on Ernst Bloch, Wayne Hudson, we could categorise this initial stage of development as Expressionist — focused on the imagination, rebelling against a culture that was seen as both stultifying and backward and yearning for something new. The first world war was a radicalising event for Bloch as it was for that entire generation of German writers, intellectuals, and artists. By 1917 Bloch was in Switzerland with a whole host of other German intellectuals, exiled from a country that seemed to have no place for him. He published his first major work, the poetic, Expressionistic book *The Spirit of Utopia*. His reputation was developing as a syncretist — someone interested in developing Marxist economics in conjunction with Biblical, Gnostic, and Romantic sources to create a whole new philosophy of life.

If the period up to 1919 was his initial Expressionist phase, from 1919–1933 Bloch turned into a forcible cultural critic, a well-regarded writer and a staunch (although never dogmatic) European Marxist. He published his study of Christian Communism on the Reformation radical, Thomas Munztner, in 1921, a work which he himself would describe as revolutionary Romanticism. Alongside this he developed links with the Frankfurt School, forming influential friendships with both Brecht and Walter Benjamin and continuing to work closely with his friend Georg Lukács. By the beginning of the 1930s he was one of the biggest defenders and advocates of modernism as a cultural form and a Marxist defender of the artistic avant-garde. But, by 1933, as fascism became more powerful and the fear mongering towards degenerate art rumbled through the German cultural landscape, Bloch would find himself a target of the Nazis and enter the third stage of his career: the intellectual in exile.

This phase would see the publication of one of Bloch's best books, *Heritage of Our Time*. It was a scathing analysis of the previous decade, sweeping across the totality of capitalist culture of the time, with even key German literary figures like Hermann Hesse praising it as the definitive analysis of the rise of fascism as both a cultural and economic force. His time in America was not easy; he spoke little English, and his colleagues and compatriots in the Frankfurt School thought Bloch far too sympathetic to the Soviets to be trusted. When peace came, Bloch returned to Germany ready to build socialism and took up the position of chair of philosophy in Leipzig, entering the fourth stage of his career — that of the (semi) institutionalised Marxist philosopher, ideologically committed to the building of socialism. He published his book on Hegel (sadly, still for the most part untranslated) and a book on what Bloch termed 'the Aristotelian left'. For a time, Bloch played the role of the loyal socialist intellectual, even being awarded the National Prize of the DDR, but his interests were too broad and his philosophical and aesthetic commitments too heterogeneous to fit comfortably into the narrow intellectual and political constraints of the DDR. As Bloch began to chafe against the restrictive atmosphere, he issued strident critiques of 'mechanical materialism'. After the seismic shock of 1956, Bloch had been unforgivably slow to offer any substantial critiques of the Stalinist terror, but was, at last, calling for a complete transformation of the philosophical and political world of East Germany. This did not go well. Bloch was forbidden from publishing, attacked in the press and his students were either jailed or forced to leave the country. He was roundly denounced as an irrationalist, a mystic and a revisionist, and he shared the fate of many great philosophers: being accused of corrupting the young.

In 1961, he was in West Germany whilst the Berlin Wall was being built and, disillusioned, he decided to stay on that side of the wall. Initially he was regarded as a throwback and a punch line — the Stalinist who finally woke up just far too late. He was too communistic for the West and not nearly communistic enough for the East. Here, he entered the fifth phase of his life, that of the revered elder philosopher. He was, eventually, awarded a guest professorship at Tübingen, the old university town of Hegel, Schelling and Holderlin and there the final phase of his life and career was one of astonishing productivity in which his work found a global audience. He was known as the old man with the raised fist, and lived to oversee the publication of his complete works.

This chapter hopefully brings some introductory context to the book; the challenge for its remainder is to explain what Bloch was up to in terms of philosophical and political commitments, and to successfully make the case for why reading Bloch now is worth the time and the effort[1]. With that as the aim, the next section functions as an exploration of one of Bloch's most famous and widely used philosophical and political terms: the 'not yet'.

Notes:

1. It's for this reason that I tried to avoid the usual style of academic writing — excessive footnotes, technical vocabulary and so on — or what Theodor Adorno would call the "tyranny of method". For those interested in sources as well as further, more academic studies on various elements of Bloch's thought and work, there is a list at the end of this book with some reading suggestions.

THE 'NOT YET', INCOMPLETENESS AND THE RETURN TO HISTORY

Our programme must be: the reform of consciousness not through dogmas but by analyzing mystical consciousness obscure to itself, whether it appear in religious or political form. It will then become plain that the world has long since dreamed of something of which it needs only to become conscious for it to possess it in reality. It will then become plain that our task is not to draw a sharp mental line between past and future, but to complete the thought of the past. Lastly, it will become plain that mankind will not begin any new work, but will consciously bring about the completion of its old work.

Letter from Karl Marx to Arnold Ruge, September 1843.

From where does philosophy begin? For some, philosophy begins with a problem: why is there something, rather than nothing? Memorably, the philosopher, Simon Critchley, argues that philosophy begins in disappointment, arising out of a kind of necessity when faced with the enormity of a world that so often seems confusing and deeply unjust. For Bloch, however, philosophy begins not with a problem, but with wonder — with the sheer astonishment of existence itself. There is, in Bloch's work, a staggering level of intellectual omnivorousness: everything means something. *Everything* is worth paying attention to. For the first-time reader approaching Bloch's magnum opus, *The Principle of Hope,* they may find it absolutely colossal, an intimidating attempt at a utopian encyclopedia of all things and a philosophical reshaping of our understanding of the universe. Yet Bloch was not just interested in the grand and hifalutin, but in the microscopic, the incidental and the fleeting. Unsurprisingly, Bloch was close friends with his compatriot, Walter Benjamin, who shared his interest in rag-picking along the flotsam and jetsam of human consciousness, picking up stories, daydreams, folk tales and stray thoughts all of which pointed us toward something. They functioned, as he put it, as *spuren,* traces of something that had to be fully understood.

Even on a more foundational level, Bloch thought we were all aware of this feeling of missing something. On the level of physiology: we hunger ergo we need food. We encounter injustice and unfairness, and we feel the possibility of justice if only by its absence. We live through the oppressions of capitalist exploitation, and we yearn for, as Bloch put it, home. In fact, this has to be put in stronger terms; our awareness of these absences underscores the extent to which what we yearn for is to be human for the first time. A genuine humanity has not yet emerged, and it was the revolutionary philosophical task of the Utopian hermeneutician to understand the process by which it *could* emerge. To quote the great Bloch scholar, Peter Thompson:

> The process that would take us from a static concept of being to one of becoming and of coming to possess ourselves was at base a material one, but it was also one in which our desires, ideas, hopes, and dreams fulfilled a fundamentally important material function in overcoming the "ontology of the not yet".

This is not simply an idealist or subjective conception of the nature of existence but a philosophically materialist one. Bloch was heavily influenced by Marx (more on Blochian politics later) but also by thinkers such as Aristotle and a materialism that saw matter as something dynamic and in process rather than as static or inert. Or, to put this another way: matter is that which is possible (determined through scientific and historical materialist conditions) but also that which can *become* possible. We are not finished, and neither is the world in which, and with which, we exist. And here we come to one of the central philosophical terms used in his recursive, modernist style: 'not yet'.

This simple phrase expresses a whole host of potential meanings — and, unsurprisingly, Bloch never found himself all that interested in straightforward definitions. Firstly, there is something that is not actually *now* but something which has a kind of actuality. The child is *not yet* an adult but possesses in that incompleteness a potential to become. Yet the term isn't just future-orientated, it can be taken to mean something like 'not so far', or even something which has failed to come to fruition. The ambiguity is stronger in the original German as Bloch's 'noch-nicht' can be translated as both not yet and still not. Here then, Bloch models a kind of Janus theory: looking back to a past in order to find the conditions, potentialities and resources by which the future might come into being — not simply historically, or even politically, but ontologically and existentially. At the same time, Bloch is looking to a future, a Utopia, which is not programmatic or deterministic, but the ever-unfolding process that is an integral part of both human nature and all of existence itself.

The consequences of this ontology of the 'not yet' are far reaching. Žižek famously draws on the 'not yet' in his own link between the fundamental incompleteness of existence with quantum mechanics. Even if you don't necessarily accept the ontological argument here — or see its relevance — the idea of the fundamental incompleteness of existence radically impacts both our conception of ideology and the role and function of history itself. Rather than try and figure out what 'really' happened in the past, the role of a Marxist and Utopian approach to the question of historiography is precisely to destabilise our certainties about history; to open up the potentialities and ambiguities of the future — of what *could be* — in our collective past. We look at the world and recognise that things did not have to be this way. The past could have been different and if we understand those moments of possibility, that opens the question of how the future can be different too. There are potentialities in the past which remain unexhausted, and it is this which explains Bloch's long interest and sympathy for religion.

Bloch was often accused of a kind of mysticism, but his interest in religion comes from his broader, philosophical commitment to the unfinished nature of our being and existence. For all its flaws, Bloch realised that religion was a profoundly future-oriented mode of living; not for nothing was he drawn to radical theologians like the German Reformation preacher, Thomas Müntzer, heralding him as the theologian of the revolution, (and it is no coincidence that Fredric Jameson rightly crowns Bloch as the closest thing the Marxist tradition has to its own theologian). Christianity spoke of a future world — a new Heaven and a New Earth — expressing in a profound and powerful way the unfinished and incomplete nature of our existence. Müntzer and figures such as the English theologian and writer, Gerrard Winstanley, saw in the religious and political systems of their own day, the possibilities of something different: of Heaven on Earth, or in more Biblical language, the Kingdom of God.

Think of Thomas Münzter's famous sermon to the princes or Gerrard Winstanley's beautiful declaration that private property was a thing founded on violence and thus an affront to God and to the world that was made as a common treasury for all people. Rather than accept an arid materialism that fell into a reductionist either/or between science and religion, Bloch's exegesis of religion was an attempt to find the materialist kernel within the ostensibly non-rational impulses of religion. As he put it, in his book *Atheism in Christianity*: 'the question here is not of giving the death-blow to fantasy as such, but of destroying and saving the myth in a single dialectical process, by shedding light upon it. What is really swept away is real superstition'. Really, religion serves as a good example of Bloch as a hermeneutical detective. Religion is a response to something, an awareness of what we are missing, a response to and cry of the 'not yet' in the world. Or, to put this in more traditional Marxist language: 'it is the sigh of the oppressed creature, the heart of a heartless world, and the soul of our soulless conditions'. Within the religious traditions of the world, we have fragments of possibility, potentialities which, if we ascribe to a strict materialism, we will miss and of which we will remain tragically ignorant. If we dismiss the sigh of the oppressed creature as false consciousness (the classic 'materialist' response) we also dismiss the possibility of liberation. Those fragments Bloch referred to as *Vorschein* (pre-appearance): something that is *there,* just beneath the surface, if we are willing to try and dig it out.

One of Bloch's principal problems with religion is in its conciliatory and pacifying impulses. The Kingdom is deferred, always still to come whereas Bloch saw the advantage of communism in its ability to *communise* the eschaton. Utopia is not simply something that is to come, some teleological moment that will arrive *eventually*. Rather, Utopia is an open-ended, processual working out of the latencies and tendencies of history, from the daydreams of the alienated worker all the way up to the great mass revolutionary struggle of the working class acting for itself, and to the physical stuff of the universe. To put it in the language of the revolutionary theology Bloch wrote of, the Kingdom of God is *at hand.* For all its still-to-come-ness Bloch described this Utopia as concrete — used in two senses. Firstly, despite its non-presence, elements of the still to come Utopia are here in some form even if we are only aware of them via their lack. Life, daily quotidian existence, has those moments of pre-appearance wherein we see, in just a moment and for a fleeting instance, what the world could be. Peter Thompson, in his introduction to *Atheism in Christianity,* puts it rather beautifully:

> Bloch's work is rich in the unbearable nearness of utopia, its
> anticipation in life and love and religion and art and culture

and music and sex and adventure and revolution: in all those moments in which we seem to go outside of ourselves and to get a glimpse of the person and the world which we could become.

Utopia is concrete in that our own shared lives are part of these processes, of the working out of the human struggle to emerge from what Bloch termed a 'pre-history'. Thus, Bloch's Utopianism is simultaneously both *speculative*, in that it points towards something which has not yet been actualised, but also *materialist* because it sees the possible fulfillment of what could come to be in the present. In the wake of the end of the end of history, the idea of the incompleteness of the present, the inexhaustible 'not yet' may no longer seem something so absurd. If we are able to look at the past with the eyes to see, we may find new potentialities in our present. The past has a cultural inheritance which has yet to be fully exhausted. Again, it's important to stress that Bloch's philosophical project is entirely within the tradition of Marx's own thought: the famous quote from *The Eighteenth Brumaire* serves as evidence:

> The tradition of all dead generations weighs like a nightmare on the brains of the living. And just as they seem to be occupied with revolutionizing themselves and things, creating something that did not exist before, precisely in such epochs of revolutionary crisis they anxiously conjure up the spirits of the past to their service, borrowing from them names, battle slogans, and costumes in order to present this new scene in world history in time-honored disguise and borrowed language. Thus, Luther put on the mask of the Apostle Paul, the Revolution of 1789–1814 draped itself alternately in the guise of the Roman Republic and the Roman Empire, and the Revolution of 1848 knew nothing better to do than to parody, now 1789, now the revolutionary tradition of 1793–95.

Marx's point was written in the context of revolutionary struggle, but in light of Bloch's expansive view on how history itself is structured, this widened out to encompass our relationship with all things, this notion of the unfinished past having possibilities with the present is the very nature of existence. After all, Bloch understood that matter is an active category — it isn't simply a 'mechanical lump' to use his own phrase, but something capable of movement and development. This is the ground of Bloch's metaphysics; a philosophy that emphasises process and renders history as something open. As Bloch put it, 'We live surrounded by possibility, not merely by presence. In the prison of mere presence we could not even move nor even breathe'.

However, this emphasis on process doesn't mean that quite literally *anything* could happen — Bloch never ascribed to a weird sort of hyper-volunteerism. We live in a historical, social, and political totality which circumscribes what is actually possible — an immediate overthrow of the American global empire is not possible under the present conditions. This is what Bloch called the objectively real-possible: that which can emerge from this present, made by this history. Yet, even with that, we cannot necessarily predict what the future might be because these broader forces do not eliminate the role of individual agency or subjective possibility.

Another couple of terms that Bloch uses are latency and tendency. Tendency is the pressures of the objectively real-possible blocked by the actual conditions of the present. This is a straightforward Marxist point put into somewhat more metaphysical terms. Bloch's famous example is the presence of the bourgeoisie in the feudal mode of production. Another good example would be the ways in which the advancements of technology which could move us beyond artificially imposed capitalist scarcity are blocked by the same forces of capitalist production. In contrast, latency is the possible content of the future that is around us. Again, Bloch uses a typically Marxist line of thinking here: the proletariat are a future revolutionary class, latent in the present and finding expression in the class struggle. These latencies of the present meet the objective real possible conditions of history and it is this that forms the dialectical engine that drives history itself forward.

All of this intersects with Bloch's understanding of consciousness which brings us onto his ideas of the 'no longer conscious' and the 'not yet conscious'. That which has dropped out of consciousness is the realm of Freud: half-memories, dreams and the points at which consciousness turns into forgetting. So much of the revolutionary symbolism of the past is now part of that shadowy realm of half-thought. In Bloch's phrasing, the 'no longer conscious' is the realm of the evening, in contrast to the 'not yet conscious', the realm of the dawn when that which previously had not been conscious comes into consciousness. It is the realm of the 'New' (always capitalised); a dawning of an unmapped world, a mode of being that is oriented towards the future.

These wider forces of history all the way down to subjective consciousness form the conditions for the emergence of the New, which Bloch terms the *Novum*. The New emerges into consciousness, mediated through those wider historical and social forces, and then has to be explicated outward into the world, becoming a kind of imminent potential: the 'not yet conscious' moving toward the 'not-yet-become'. A vital aspect of Bloch's philosophy of history is our inability to properly grasp either ourselves or the true state of the present moment. Bloch wrote often of the darkness of the lived moment, and in an interview said that 'at the foot of the lighthouse, there is no light'. What might the present be? Without action, a dark void, but with an understanding of the 'not yet' the present becomes a drive towards something still to be made, a revolutionary movement from the 'not yet' to Utopia coming into being.

One of the issues with too strict a commitment to a totalised understanding of capitalism is that it can presuppose a universalism to the experiences of capitalism on a day-to-day level that is simply not true. Or, as Bloch would put it, we do not all inhabit the same *Now*. Bloch used the term *Ungleichzeitigkeit*, usually translated as the non-synchronous to articulate the fundamental incompleteness of the capitalist revolution; that what can be taken for the naturalised state of things is never complete and can vary greatly depending upon one's class position, community, and location. For Bloch it was this non-synchronicity which was key to explaining the ways in which various strata of German class society were recruited to the fascist cause and Bloch's political analysis more generally. The idea of the non-synchronic draws off earlier work, going to Marx himself on uneven development in capitalist economics, but Bloch was interested in understanding how this unevenness had political, sociological, and cultural impact. Capitalism depends upon *churn*, a consistent cacophony of change and never-ending production. It will never be done, never be finished. In China Mieville's words, 'capitalism is catastrophe, exhausting, brutal, quite unrelenting, it just will not give us a minute, and it is too fucking loud'.

But, as Bloch pointed out, not only is the capitalist Now never a standardised and finalised whole, but this incompleteness needs to be extended into how Marxists understand history and dialectical processes. The whole purpose of the non-synchronous as an idea is to work against a vulgar Marxist teleology of history, with its over-determination and reliance on schematised stages of history. History is not finished, the present is incomplete, and the future is still to be determined and as should be established by now; one of Bloch's central philosophical claims here is that this is true of the past too. As Bloch puts it in his typically loquacious prose:

> [O]ne ... gains additional revolutionary force from the incomplete wealth of the past, especially if it is not "sublated" in the last stage. The still subversive and utopian contents in the relations of people to people and nature, which are not past because they were never quite attained, can only be of use in this way. These contents are, as it were, the gold-bearing gravel in the course of previous labor processes and their superstructures in the form of works. Polyphonous dialectics, as a dialectics of the "contradictions" which are more concentrated today than ever, has in any case enough questions

and contents in capitalism that are not yet "superseded by the course of economic development." The proletarian voice of synchronous dialectics remains decidedly the leading one; but both above and below this cantus firmus [fixed hymn] run disorderly emissions which can only be related to the cantus firmus [fixed hymn] by its relating itself to them in a critical and non-contemplative totality.

Bloch's concept of the non-synchronous then allows for an understanding of history as a potential source of revolutionary power, building for us a greater appreciation of the Now in all its possibilities and conjunctions. To put this in more Gothic terminology, the capitalist present is haunted twofold, by both its own internal and contradictory non-synchronicity and the broader inescapable hauntings of history, riddled with un-exorcised monsters whose shadows linger, revealing the fundamental incompleteness of capitalist hegemony and the possibility of their return. Things can seem so bleak, history so empty of content, the shock of the New such a distant memory that the possibility of some radical break or rupture towards the Utopian (or even just for the better) can all too easily simply come off as naive optimism. However, Bloch's point about non-synchronicity shows us that the past is in some way still with us, we live in its ruins and from those ruins the future is not something enforced by teleological systems but is something made and remade too.

MARXISM AND THE POLITICS OF UTOPIAN STRUGGLE

For all our contemporary anxieties around mainstream politics, Bloch's own political development deserves some attention. Bloch came to Utopian and Marxist politics in 1920s and 1930s Germany, in the midst of the rise of violent fascism. Thus, for the Utopian Bloch, his own politics had to respond to the material conditions and social totality of his own day. If any kind of Marxism faces challenges now, in the conditions of capitalist realism, then this is not a challenge of which Bloch himself was ignorant. As with his broader intellectual trajectory, perhaps it's best to deal with Bloch's own politics in stages. Firstly, his early work is a romantic and humanist rejection of what he saw as a stultifying historical materialism in Marxism. In historical materialism, wondered the young Bloch, where was the space of the individual, for the particularity of lived experience and the subjective yearning for something new? There's a famous quote from the second edition of *The Spirit of Utopia* that underscores the early Bloch's dissatisfaction:

> People, not things and not the mighty course of events outside ourselves (which Marx falsely places above us), write history. His determinism applies to the economic future, to the

necessary economic-institutional change; but the new man, the leap, the power of love and life, and morality itself, are not yet accorded the requisite independence in the definitive social order.

Whilst the Marxologists will happily debate the accuracy of Bloch's point, it's not a surprising one for a young man who came of age in the post-Nietzschean, expressionist, artistic and intellectual atmosphere of the late-nineteenth and early-twentieth-century Germany. He was a Messianic youth with a head full of Tolstoy and Dostoevsky and nothing but contempt for the institutions of the time. His early work staged a fierce critique of the astringent, stultifying rationalism of the time. Here he followed the intellectual influence of Schelling: thought was not the same thing as Being and the idea that the world was given to consciousness as nothing but concepts was one he rejected. The world was not simply given, at hand and easily solved, but was something that came to our consciousness through unfolding processes.

To put this another way, the world is essentially problematic and needs explanation. Or, in language that Existential philosophers would recognize, Appearance is not Essence and the task of humanity is that of completing the incompleteness of existence itself. Here we can see a proto-Messianism and the centrality of the role of ordinary humanity. Yet later his friend and intellectual comrade, Lukács, would point out that Bloch had not yet appreciated the full depth of dialectical and historical materialism. Bloch's next stage of intellectual development then is to re-orientate his understanding of Marx not as an insufficient system of thought but as the fulfillment of all other previously insufficient systems, carrying on and instantiating on firm foundations the revolutionary work of Joachim of Fiore, of Thomas Müntzer, of Goethe, of Faust and all the heretics of history. Bloch's Marxism then, is a humanist Marxism, seeing Karl as the subjective genius who mediates the objective 'not yet conscious' of that which is beyond capitalism more generally. But it is an active humanism that hates oppressors and lays the basis for the action necessary to bring that oppression to an end. If you want to be a little less charitable, it could be claimed that Bloch simply grafted his own idealist and expressionist philosophy into a Marxist framework — a kind of intellectual conversion experience — but at the very least, his Marxism is the antithesis of deterministic, arid, or teleological materialism. As he would later write in *The Principle of Hope,* Marxism is nothing less than the struggle against dehumanisation and the promotion of humanity. Importantly, Bloch took not just from Marx but from the great philosopher of the bourgeoisie: Hegel.

Bloch's Hegelianism, like all his intellectual interests, was never straightforward. He was attracted to Hegel for the focus on process, following Marx and Engels in discarding the world spirit and understanding dialectics as a material process. However, unlike others who try and strip out the inconvenient theology and mysticism in Hegel, Bloch saw him as both a Rosicrucian and a gnostic, someone who was methodologically in the tradition of thinkers such as Aristotle, Plotinus, Nicholas of Cusa, Boehme and Leibniz. Reality is a subject-object process, and it is this thought which aims at solving the problems created through the divide of an objective reality and subjective experience. Bloch's relationship to Hegel is complex, but perhaps can be best summed up by pointing out that if Marx placed Hegel's dialectic the right way up, Bloch thought that Marxism had to do the same thing for the entirety of Hegel's philosophical system. Bloch used the term *Umfunktionierung* (repurposing) to describe the relation between Marxism and Hegel. Marxism has to take on Hegel's ideas of totality and his encyclopedia of the world in thought: not to Hegelianise Marx, but to utopianise Hegel.

Contra to Althusser and some other European Marxists of the middle and late-twentieth century, Bloch rejects any sense of a split between the earlier humanist and later anti-humanist Marx. Marx could not be split in half, as he put it. Rather, revolution is the fulfillment of humanity, representing the shift from an abstract humanism (or humanism in theory, as we might put it) to a concrete humanism, put into praxis. Here then we start to see the shapes of Bloch's politics in their mature phase: committed to revolutionary struggle, humanist, and philosophically indebted to Hegel and to the wider tradition of German idealism. The letter from Marx to Ruge that I quoted near the beginning is one of which Bloch himself was very fond, expressing as it does what he saw as Marxism's own understanding of the future-in-the-past, the revolutionary potential that runs throughout all human history. History was not a temple of memory. To use Bloch's phrase: history, transformed by Marxism, was an *arsenal*. What makes Marxism so essential for Bloch is its ability to mediate the often-inchoate Utopian longing of the 'not yet' with the concrete struggle of how to bring these things into being. As Bloch put it in a rather beautiful phrase in the final third of *The Principle of Hope*: 'Reason cannot blossom without hope, hope cannot speak without reason, both in Marxist unity — no other science has any future, no other future any science'. This brings up one of Bloch's other favorite phrases: the cold and warm streams of Marxism, or the two ways of Being Red. The cold stream of Marxism is that of clear, rigorous analysis — a focus on political economy and on capital: quantifiable and precise. The warm stream of Marxism is that of the prophet crying in the wilderness. It is the intuitive awareness of the unfairness of capitalism, the desire and joy for a world of justice and abundance for all, and for the liberation of humanity from the drudgery of exploitative labor.

Importantly for Bloch, one could not have one of these streams of thought without the other, certainly not without incurring some major problems. The cold stream of Marxism without the imaginative and creative spark of the warm stream led to empty, hollow materialism: a hectoring Marxism that had little to say about things like religion, or culture, beyond a dismissal of its false consciousness. This was the Marxism that Bloch could be utterly scathing about: an imaginatively malnourished Socialism which had nothing to say of ideals, of enthusiasm or of the real needs of ordinary people. On the other hand, Marxism without some careful, cold, and sober analysis risks a descent into a kind of revolutionary fanaticism where the active process of revolution instead becomes revenge. Only with these two forces, these two essential structures of feeling held in a delicate homeostasis could Marxism become the Utopian philosophy it was meant to be: or, as Bloch put it, only Marxism is both detective and liberator.

Again, in the context of his own time, the argument he was making was a bold one. He saw the communists of his day as absolutely insufficient to face up to fascism and his own political philosophy offered a novel explanation of why the fascists in Germany were so successful. Rather than simply label the upsurge in Romanticism, Nationalism, and occultism as a kind of irrationalism and the rise of fascism as simply the long overdue decay of the bourgeoisie, Bloch argued that emergent fascism had to be understood as a political synthesis and a twisted revolution; a swindle of fulfillment to use his own terms. Bloch also rejected the Freudian line on fascism that it was, in some ways, incipient within German psychology. Rather, Bloch argued that fascism spoke to the non-synchronous, non-contemporaneous contradictions of German society in the language of dreams, hopes and fantasies whereas too much of the Marxism of the day had nothing to say beyond chastisement for irrationalism. This allows us to form a clear idea of what Marxism itself was to Bloch. It was not a search for a perfect theory, or another positivistic science. Marxism was the philosophy of revolution and must necessarily be involved in the ongoing development of a given society and must bring all of the potentially progressive elements of a social totality into its own organising structures. For all their fetishised, abstract rationalism, Bloch thought these Marxists were functionally irrational themselves, unwilling to confront the world as it truly was. Marxism had to be willing and able to occupy the political imagination, the space of culture, of dreaming and of fantasy. Firstly, Marxism was a retroactive baptism of the unfinished past by bringing all the superstition and fragments of history to bear towards a rationally grounded hope for the future and secondly, Marxism needed a theology. What Bloch means is a way of orienting imagination, enthusiasm and thought toward revolutionary Utopia. (Not for nothing does Fredric Jameson point out that if the critique about Marxism being a religion has a grain of truth to it, then so too does the opposite — that all religions are perhaps uncomfortably close to Marxism!)

This task was essential for at least two reasons: firstly, it is a task that capitalism itself is incapable of even attempting. As *The Communist Manifesto* puts it, all that is solid melts into air, all that is holy is profaned. Capitalism will liquidate everything to the subordination of commodification; there is at the very heart of the capitalist process a hollow void. Secondly, if the communists cannot occupy that space, then the forces of reaction absolutely will. In a way, Bloch's Marxism is a Marxist critique of Marxism, trying to make Marxism into not a science, but thought which can speak to every aspect of human life and a philosophical, Utopian political practice. However, this raises a problem, which is the seeming contradiction and challenges of reconciling Marxism and Utopia. The standard objection to Utopia rests upon three criticisms: ontological, regional, and psychological. Firstly, the nature of things is just given; or, in other words, the utopian thinker denies the material reality with which they are confronted. Secondly, the regional problem is that Utopia is not here and now but located somewhere else. Finally, and perhaps most worryingly, Utopianism leads to a kind of psychological subjectivism. Utopianism refuses to recognise the possibility of failure and even absolute disaster in the pursuit of the good. Utopianism is, so the charge goes, about impotently trying to remake the world and blithely ignoring all the horrors that can come along with this. (This is, I think, an argument restaged in more modern language in the work of someone like the Canadian podcaster and psychologist Jordan B Peterson, but, even just at a minimum, Peterson and those like him ignore the possibility of pragmatic and non-violent change to society.)

Bloch deals with these three criticisms by denying the premise for each of them. Firstly, let's deal with that first criticism that Utopianism involves a denial of the nature of reality. A crucial part of Bloch's entire body of thought is his own concept of matter as process. Bloch takes Aristotle's notion of entelechy, that within all things is a kind of potential becoming. The seed of the flower is never just the seed but contains within itself the fullness of the flower in bloom. Material reality is not something simply given, and as such, Utopia is fundamental to the unfinished nature of existence. As Bloch put it himself: there is no realism worthy of the name, which abstracts from this strongest element in reality as something which is unfinished. This is not simply a philosophical point but also extends to both Bloch's politics and conception of history, explaining Bloch's own rejection of this regionalist criticism mentioned above. Bloch's own philosophy of history argued for a proleptic understanding of existence in which the past was still with us, and the future here in fleeting glimpses of what could be. Wayne Hudson explains Bloch's point like this: 'the far is present in the near, and the problem of the identification and realisation of what is needed is not only a problem of our relationship to the external world and its possibility content, but a problem of our relationship to the now of the lived moment'. The final point is that Bloch denies that Utopianism involves a departure from reality. For Bloch, this is perhaps at best only half true but is an undialectical criticism which ignores the ways in which utopia has a heuristic function, uncovering new ideas, new possibilities, and new modes of life. These new modes of life should not be discounted simply because they represent a break from what we take to just be the way things are. Utopia is a philosophical and ontological rupture, and it is a damning indictment of our own current imaginative and intellectual malnourishment that such a rupture is for many, quite literally unthinkable.

From this outline, Bloch can be seen as a thinker in constant motion: a Marxist heretic who avoided the idea of a program or a search for the perfect theory. Rather, his revolutionary politics were bound up with his philosophical commitment to process philosophy. 'Processus cum figures, figurae in processu' as he was fond of saying: the process is made by those who are made by the process. There is no telos, no program or revolutionary committee which can enforce Utopia on us — the perfect State will not make it happen nor will the dictates of a Church point us the right way. Rather, Utopia is *made*, an open-ended and auto-poetic process embodied by the labouring, struggling, dreaming working classes. Throughout so much of Bloch's work it is the proletariat, the working classes that are the focus of Utopian and revolutionary activity. Those who often have no time or freedom but that which can be dreamed and fantasised about, are perhaps the most attuned to the latencies and possibilities of the present moment: the short, fleeting glimpses of what the world could be, beyond the limits of labour.

Throughout the whole range of Bloch's work, it was the proletariat that represented that revolutionary hope and he always kept faith with Marx's idea of the 'Universal Class'. However, this does represent something of a problem that has to be overcome. Bloch's work speaks of the multiplicity of revolutionary potential that exists across all strata of society, so to emphasise one class at the expense of another does create some friction with the polyphonic dialectical mode of analysis that he practiced. Bloch offered a choral metaphor in *Heritage of Our Times* that shows his own way through the problem:

> The proletarian voice of the contemporaneous dialectic firmly remains the leading one; yet beneath and above this cantus firmus there run disordered exuberances which are to be referred to the cantus firmus only through the fact that the latter – in critical and non-contemplative totality – refers to them.

If the contemporaneous contradiction in capitalism is on the subjective level, the revolutionary activity of the proletariat, then the objective expression of this contradiction is the embryonic socialism that is already present here in capitalism. Marxist strategy has to try to bind up one with the other, because it is only in the harmonious song of both that there remains the possibility of the negation of the negation and the emergence of the New. The danger, of course, is in the collapse of the dialectical tension between the revolutionary discipline of proletarian struggle and the latent possibility of the 'not yet'. Without the anchoring of the working classes, Utopian struggle collapses into a naive liberalism, a celebration that reduces things down to the equation: Utopia = when good things happen to me and others I like. Too often this seems like the contemporary problem that philosophical and political Utopianism suffers from. If, in Bloch's writing, the great worry was the paucity and malnourishment of our imagination, Utopianism today suffers from both a restricted imagination and an absence of militant organisation that could channel the imaginative dreams of the future towards concrete goals. The struggle now is not for Utopia; rather our position — far bleaker — is to try and make Utopianism *thinkable* in the terms that Bloch outlines.

THE PRINCIPLE OF HOPE: DREAMS OF A BETTER LIFE

'We must believe in the Principle of Hope. A Marxist does not have the right to be a pessimist'

When the Nazis rose to power, Bloch found himself on a list of intellectuals and troublemakers for arrest. Like many of his generation he made his way to the United States. He arrived there in 1938 and would stay there for the next decade or so along with his wife, the architect and socialist, Karola Piotrkowska. Unlike many of his colleagues from the Frankfurt School he was seen as too Marxist to be acceptable and found life in the USA very difficult. He had no permanent academic position, few contacts who were not German émigrés and he spoke very little English and was generally isolated from other German intellectuals. Bloch's communism also meant he was met with some suspicion in the USA, regularly forced to appear at the immigration office in Boston to see whether he was fit to be American. He was even forced to undergo an examination on the American constitution: in a fun (though possibly not true) detail, his wife tells of how his examiners listened, rapt, to Bloch's own extemporaneous analysis of the American War of Independence and that was how he gained his citizenship. And so, in the Harvard library over the course of a decade or so, he pieced together the thousands of pages that would become *The Principle of Hope*.

The book in its English translation spans 3 volumes and some 1600 pages. It covers everything from daydreams to new dance movements, Marxist exegesis to philosophical riffs on Hegel. In a revealing (but honestly, very funny) detail, the introduction to the first volume of the English translation notes that it is an unabashedly literary work, which, as the translators put it, explains why the book was received with skepticism by Marxists. But the initial problem for the first-time reader absolutely is one of style — Bloch uses proverbs, quotes and references, and philosophical terms drawn from Greek, Latin and German philosophy freely. That said, it's often a difficult but undeniably exhilarating experience to read it. And, to borrow a line of thought from Adorno, the style is not something to get over but rather the very first step on grasping what Bloch is doing. The bafflement, confusion, or frustration a first-time reader feels is not something to shy away from; we need to be shaken out of our old ways of thinking and it is this which the style of *The Principle of Hope* aims to do. The book represents the crowning achievement of Bloch's own philosophical project and the place in which you see the fullest articulation of his entire aesthetics. What Bloch is trying to do is excavate all of history, to comb through the sum of all things and find here, there and everywhere, the traces of the 'not yet conscious'. He wants to bring us to a remembrance of the future in the past and, at the same time, place his central concepts of the 'not yet' as a philosophical and metaphysical fulcrum for all human existence. For all its florid language the opening pages are, for Bloch at least, remarkably systematic. He begins with a series of questions: Who are we? Where do we come from? Where are we going? What are we waiting for? What awaits us? The aim of these is to orient the reader, by taking us on a tour of human history; through philosophy and revolutionary politics we might be returned to ourselves, transformed. The challenge Bloch throws down at the opening of the book is that of 'venturing beyond'. His aim is the instantiation and recuperation of the forward dream — the dream that is yet to come into being. Or, to quote Bloch directly:

> Hope, with its positive correlate: the still unclosed determinateness of existence, superior to any res finita, does not therefore occur in the history of the sciences, either as psychological or as cosmic entity and least of all as functionary of what has never been, of the possible New. Therefore: a particularly extensive attempt is made in this book to bring philosophy to hope, as to a place in the world which is as inhabited as the best civilized land and as unexplored as the Antarctic.

So, how is a reader supposed to engage with this process — a book which is trying to carve out a whole new land of thought? Happily, while the book's content is dense and the scope of the argument is astonishingly ambitious, the structure of the book is far more approachable. It's broken into vignettes of a sort, moving through the various layers of consciousness and experience in which we might see glimpses of the 'not yet conscious'. He begins at the very start with incidental daydreams: what do you hope for in the unguarded moments of your own mind? How does that change as we age? What's so refreshing about Bloch is far from seeing all this as basic or essentially trivial, these tiny moments of human development can tell us so much about what it is we want. The very first section of *The Principle of Hope* reads, in its entirety, as follows:

1.
We Start Out Empty.
I move. From early on we are searching. All we do is crave, cry out. We do not have what we want.

Once again, in Bloch's work there is this existential problem — this gap, a darkness of the lived moment from which we are forced to move. We feel within ourselves a great need, and, to go even further, we do not yet even know who or what we are. Right at the beginning of the third volume of the English translation, Bloch puts it like this:

> From early on we want to get to ourselves. But we do not know who we are. All that seems clear is that nobody is what he would like to be or could be. Hence the common envy, namely of those who seem to have, in fact to be, what we are entitled to. But hence also the desire to start something new which begins with ourselves. Attempts have always been made to live commensurately with ourselves. We have in us what we could become.

In a sense, we are pushed into the future through this dialectical tension and, on the collective level, the incompleteness and inexhaustible nature of our own shared history is both a resource and catalyst for a shared process of struggle. I think in the age of capitalist realism, Bloch's injunction against pessimism might strike the reader as slightly odd, a willful denial of the facts. Yet, what interests me about the claim is the use of the word 'right'. Pessimism is a *choice*. A choice for what, to do what? I think if we idealise the concept of pessimism, we think of it as a cold-hearted appraisal of just what *is*. And it is this which I think is precisely Bloch's problem with pessimism — it involves choosing to settle for the facts in front of us and choosing not to see the latencies and possibilities *within* those facts. If hope is the philosophy of the future, then pessimism is about the abnegation of the future. Really, the pessimist sees only the NOW at the cost of the NOVUM. The Marxist has a responsibility to be the one who looks beyond the mere appearance of reality to both accept and take on its incompleteness. *The Principle of Hope* points out that through all of history there is no such thing as just the way things are and so, if we have new ways of reading our present, from there we can begin building out the shared processes of concrete Utopia. As Bloch puts it at the end of Atheism in Christianity:

Far from being a contradiction in terms, concrete Utopia is the firmest of handholds, and by no means only where the propaganda and implementation of socialism is concerned. The whole surplus force of culture finds its salvation there, and these forces are becoming more and more relevant to us all the time.

Originally, *The Principle of Hope* was supposed to have a different title: 'Dreams of A Better Life'. Can I ask something of you? Wherever you are, close your eyes, just for a moment. What do you dream of? Do you have the dreams of a better life — the unshakeable feeling that **the world is not right?** The beautiful and comforting thing about Bloch's crowning achievement is the philosophical commitment to the simple truth that those dreams mean something, and that they are the ground on which we all may find a greater world, yet to come into being. The great joy and inspiration of reading Bloch's work, and perhaps *The Principle of Hope* particularly, is a kind of cross-historical solidarity. To look at the world and see that it could be otherwise can be a profoundly lonely and isolating experience, especially under the psychic weight of a capitalist realism that drives home the message that there is no alternative, that reality is closed and the horizon of possibility has collapsed. Facing an ever-escalating series of crises, we are in such desperate need of the Promethean idea of Blochian Marxism that can re-awaken the sense of potential within our shared and collective agency.

The sweep of Bloch's argument is completely extraordinary, moving from the smallest moments of our own consciousness to art, religion, literature, and philosophy from across the world, attempting to map the shifts in both subjective consciousness and the objective material totality in which we live, work and struggle. Perhaps then it is worth thinking about the idea of Utopia in the present age. Bloch was a poet, prophet and philosopher who saw that Utopia was not an eschatology; not a place, but a guided, grounded process that required us to give up so many of our preconceived notions. To rescue and resuscitate the idea of Utopia in the contemporary moment is a colossal challenge. We are, as Bloch pointed out, strangers to ourselves, or, in other words, we do not yet remember what we are capable of. The reasons for this are both external and internal — after all, capitalist realism is as much an economic reality as it is global *Weltanschauung*, a structure of feeling that both mediates political and social externalities as at the same time it shapes us existentially and psychologically as subjects. Within ourselves we have not just conscious drives towards a future but also unconscious drives. These unspoken desires were the ground of the New, from the politics of a mass movement to the fleeting dreams of someone trapped in what David Graeber calls a bullshit job. The psychiatrist and phenomenologist, Thomas Fuchs, pointed out a few other common phenomena which fit Bloch's conception of the 'not yet conscious' ranging from words and names being on the tip of one's tongue, to inchoate impulses and desires which have yet to find full expression. Bloch understood the 'not yet conscious' as a historical force but also as a psychological truth about individuals. Yet, on the subjective level it seems that the 'not yet conscious' is not known or even acknowledged. But, as Bloch pointed out this is not a new problem. In *The Principle of Hope* he talks of the newness of our self-understanding, that only in the past two centuries have we started to plumb the depth of the mind. Bloch's rather scathing criticism of Freud and Jung particularly, are worth noting here. Bloch found their insistent focus on connecting the unconscious with the past politically unforgivable. The point, for Bloch, is not suppression and repression but rather the liberatory and revolutionary possibilities of the 'not yet conscious' coming into being. For Bloch, there was nothing new in the Freudian unconscious. Not for nothing did he dismiss Jung as a psychoanalytic fascist. Rather, via Leibniz, Bloch terms the unconscious as the source of 'petite perceptions', which emerged through *Sturm und Drang* and German Romanticism in a flood of artistic creativity and insight. But this promising movement in art and culture was stamped out by the reactionary bourgeois

Romantics and the depth psychologists like Jung. Rather, what is needed is a model of hermeneutics which can move between both the subjective and the universal, or the Subject and the Object and mediate the movement of the 'not yet conscious' into full Being.

For that, Bloch argues, we need imagination. We need art that can give expression to the possibilities and that which is 'not yet'. Bloch puts it rather neatly here in Volume One of *The Principle of Hope*:

> Its contents are first represented in ideas, and essentially in those of the imagination. In imaginative ideas, as opposed to those remembered ones which merely reproduce past perceptions and thereby shade off more and more into the past. And even these imaginative ideas are not ones which are merely composed of existing material, in arbitrary fashion (stony sea, golden mountain and so on), but extend, in an anticipating way, existing material into the future possibilities of being different and better.

How little of contemporary culture has the courage to do this! In cinema, the mainstream languishes in the ruins of pseudo-liberal hero movies where all things aim toward the restoration of the status quo. For any Utopian, the imperative of cultural critique is in the defense and promotion of the New — hunting out the possibilities and potentialities that show promise. For that reason, *The Principle of Hope* is an invaluable and too-little-used guidebook, a tool to show us now the resources we have forgotten we have to hand.

FINAL WORDS: GENESIS AT THE END

Hic Rhodus, hic saltus. *To apprehend what is is the task of philosophy, because what is is reason. As for the individual, every one is a son of his time; so philosophy also is its time apprehended in thoughts. It is just as foolish to fancy that any philosophy can transcend its present world, as that an individual could leap out of his time or jump over Rhodes. If a theory transgresses its time, and builds up a world as it ought to be, it has an existence merely in the unstable element of opinion, which gives room to every wandering fancy. With little change the above saying would read: Here is the rose, here dance.*

G.W.F. Hegel, preface to the *Philosophy of Right*

Utopia is imperative. For some this claim will be too strong; a succumbing to either a naivety or a refusal to look at the facts. But to ignore the possibility of rupture, to foreclose reality into the closed system of capitalist hegemony is to give our enemies too much credit and to ignore the ever-present possibilities all around us. Any kind of Marxism must be practical after all, and Utopianism is a flight of fancy that must be discarded for the long slog of dealing with the world as it is. Midway through the first volume of *The Principle of Hope* Bloch offers a genuinely stunning rebuttal, well worth quoting at length:

Pure wishful thinking has discredited utopias for centuries, both in pragmatic political terms and in all other expressions of what is desirable; just as if every utopia were an abstract one. And undoubtedly the utopian function is only immaturely present in abstract utopianizing, i.e. still predominantly without solid subject behind it and without relation to the Real-Possible ... But at least as suspicious as the immaturity (fanaticism) of the undeveloped utopian function is the widespread and ripe old platitude of the way-of-the-world philistine, of the blinkered empiricist whose world is far from being a stage, in short, the confederacy in which the fat bourgeois and the shallow practicist have always not only rejected outright the anticipatory, but despised it.

For Bloch, Utopia, even in its most nascent, abstract, and underdeveloped forms, is worth something — a brief, flickering glimpse of a potential future seen through a glass darkly. The point is not to dispel the illusion but to provide a process by which those anticipatory dreams and small illuminations find means of being made manifest or realised in the world. The alternative is so much worse; a cynical capitulation to this world and a forsaking of the future. Bloch's scathing point about the way-of-the-world philistine, whose world is far from being a stage, is one well worth internalising. To see the world as a stage is to see the course of events as still essentially open to change — after all, to be an actor on a stage, is to be able to *act*. When the stakes are so immeasurably high for us all, and the possibilities of disaster and death are ever more starkly clear, this is a possibility we should cling to with all our strength. The small, reformist changes will not save us, and the great Utopian gamble is the only thing that might — might — come close to doing so. Hope is something more than just a subjective feeling, but a fundamental re-orientation of our whole Being, both on the level of the individual and on the grounding of a class struggle. At every point Bloch drives home the point that Marxism is both the organisation of the present and at the same time, the venturing beyond what is, to bring something new into being in language redolent with both poetry and the imagery of the Old Testament.

As Bloch puts it: 'the very power and truth of Marxism consists in the fact that it has driven the cloud in our dreams further forward, but has not extinguished the pillar of fire in those dreams, rather strengthened it with concreteness. Thus, the utopian function is also the only transcendent one which has remained, and the only one which deserves to remain: one which is transcendent without transcendence. Consciousness of the Front provides the best light for this utopian function as the comprehended activity of the expectant emotion, of the hope-premonition, maintains the alliance with all that is still morning-like in the world. Utopian function thus understands what is exploding, because it is this itself in a very condensed way: its Ratio is the unweakened Ratio of a militant optimism. Therefore: the act-content of hope is, as a consciously illuminated, knowingly elucidated content, the positive utopian function. The historical content of hope, first represented in ideas, encyclopedically explored in real judgements, is human culture referred to its concrete utopian horizon.'

What is Utopia? It is no place, nor program, nor Party. It is rather the *concrescere* — the growing together of the often-inchoate dreams and yearning and suffering of all things. We've all had moments in life that touch upon eternity. Brief snatches of time wherein the sky lightens, and the unmistakable feeling is that of 'why can't life always be like this?' You'll find those moments in protests, on picket lines, in occupations, and in all struggles for freedom and liberation expressed through the creative agency and action of all peoples. The moments where feeling and knowledge seemingly come together, when human culture refers itself to that Utopian horizon are the times which can radicalise people into the militant commitment of which Bloch speaks in the passage above. What is needed is not yet more sober-minded recitations of the way things are — the situation is on every front ever-more bleak, this we know. However, all the diagnosis of the present and the elucidation of the problems we face on every front must be infused with the spirit of Utopia: the hermeneutics and politics that allow us to see beyond the Present. Bloch constantly warns against getting lost in abstract wish-fulfillment, but the Utopian challenge is to hold these two things in a productive, dialectical tension, combining an understanding of our conditions and at the same time understanding our still to be realized potential.

In the wake of defeats, disasters, and setbacks the Utopian imagination has perhaps never been so needed and yet so utterly starved. It is from here that we have to begin, for if the revolutionary struggle of moving beyond the annihilationism of contemporary capitalism will continue, we must find new ways of thinking and dreaming and imagining the world beyond it. Marx may have warned against developing speculative programs for the future, but Bloch's work allows us to fully grasp the totality of our current historical and social conjuncture and at the same time see within the present, the seeds of the future, waiting to germinate. There is the old adage now on the left that it is easier to imagine the end of the world than the end of capitalism. I can think of no better way of expressing the depth of our problems than the incontrovertible truth of that sentence. Yet even here, the Utopian surplus of existence and the stirring of the 'not yet conscious' can be felt and understood, even in the most surprising circumstances. To develop our capacity for imagination is perhaps one of the most urgent first steps of renewing the Utopian tradition. May the work of Ernst Bloch add some powerful fuel to that fire.

Here is the rose, here dance!

SUGGESTED FURTHER READING AND SOURCES

Bloch, Ernst, *Atheism in Christianity*. A groundbreaking work of atheist, Marxist theology providing one of the best expositions of the Utopian potential in the Christian religion tradition.

Bloch, Ernst, (trans. Neville Plaice, Stephen Plaice and Paul Knight), *The Principle of Hope*. Three volumes. The capstone to Bloch's entire oeuvre and a colossal achievement of European twentieth-century philosophy.

Geoghegan, Vincent, *Ernst Bloch*. A thorough and well-researched intellectual biography, which is perhaps a little too quick to label Bloch a Stalinist, but the section on Bloch's philosophy of law is extremely important.

Hudson, Wayne, *The Marxist Philosophy of Ernst Bloch*. An essential and readable introduction to Bloch's work and context that places a welcome emphasis on Bloch's unorthodox, militant Marxism.

Jameson, Fredric, *Marxism and Form*. One of Jameson's earliest books and still a classic. The chapter on Bloch did much to popularise his work and if you are looking for a place to start, start here.

Moir, Cat, *Ernst Bloch's Speculative Materialism: Ontology, Epistemology, Politics*. A newer book on Bloch which places him into the tradition of speculative materialism, drawing off Bloch's (sadly untranslated) book on materialism.

Thompson, Peter and Zikek, Slavoj (eds.), *The Privatization of Hope: Ernst Bloch and The Future of Utopia*. A collection of essays from contemporary writers on Bloch covering poetics, politics and much more.

CULTURE, SOCIETY & POLITICS

Contemporary culture has eliminated the concept and public
figure of the intellectual. A cretinous anti-intellectualism
presides, cheer-led by hacks in the pay of multinational
corporations who reassure their bored readers that there is no
need to rouse themselves from their stupor. Zer0 Books knows
that another kind of discourse — intellectual without being
academic, popular without being populist — is not only possible
but already flourishing. Zer0 is convinced that in the unthinking,
blandly consensual culture in which we live, critical and
engaged theoretical reflection is more important
than ever before.
If you have enjoyed this book, why not tell other readers by
posting a review on your preferred book site.
You may also wish to
subscribe to our Zer0 Books YouTube Channel.

Bestsellers from Zer0 Books include:

Poor but Sexy
Culture Clashes in Europe East and West
Agata Pyzik
How the East stayed East and the West stayed West.
Paperback:978-1-78099-394-2 ebook: 978-1-78099-395-9

An Anthropology of Nothing in Particular
Martin Demant Frederiksen
A journey into the social lives of meaninglessness.
Paperback: 978-1-78535-699-5 ebook: 978-1-78535-700-8

In the Dust of This Planet
Horror of Philosophy vol. 1
Eugene Thacker
In the first of a series of three books on the Horror of Philosophy,
In the Dust of This Planet offers the genre of horror as a way of
thinking about the unthinkable.
Paperback: 978-1-84694-676-9 ebook: 978-1-78099-010-1

The End of Oulipo?
An Attempt to Exhaust a Movement
Lauren Elkin, Veronica Esposito
Paperback: 978-1-78099-655-4 ebook: 978-1-78099-656-1

Capitalist Realism
Is There No Alternative?
Mark Fisher
An analysis of the ways in which capitalism has presented itself
as the only realistic political-economic system.
Paperback: 978-1-84694-317-1 ebook: 978-1-78099-734-6

Rebel Rebel
Chris O'Leary
David Bowie: every single song. Everything you want to know,
everything you didn't know.
Paperback: 978-1-78099-244-0 ebook: 978-1-78099-713-1

Cartographies of the Absolute
Alberto Toscano, Jeff Kinkle
An aesthetics of the economy for the twenty-fi rst century.
Paperback: 978-1-78099-275-4 ebook: 978-1-78279-973-3

Malign Velocities
Accelerationism and Capitalism
Benjamin Noys
Long listed for the Bread and Roses Prize 2015, *Malign Velocities*
argues against the need for speed, tracking acceleration
as the symptom of the ongoing crises of capitalism.
Paperback: 978-1-78279-300-7 ebook: 978-1-78279-299-4

Babbling Corpse
Vaporwave and the Commodifi cation of Ghosts
Grafton Tanner
Paperback: 978-1-78279-759-3 ebook: 978-1-78279-760-9

New Work New Culture
Work we want and a culture that strengthens us
Frithjof Bergmann
A serious alternative for humankind and the planet.
Paperback: 978-1-78904-064-7 ebook: 978-1-78904-065-4

Romeo and Juliet in Palestine
Teaching Under Occupation
Tom Sperlinger
Life in the West Bank, the nature of pedagogy and the role of a
university under occupation.
Paperback: 978-1-78279-637-4 ebook: 978-1-78279-636-7

Color, Facture, Art and Design
Iona Singh
This materialist definition of fine art develops guidelines for
architecture, design, cultural studies, and ultimately, social
change.
Paperback: 978-1-78099-629-5 ebook: 978-1-78099-630-1

Sweetening the Pill
or How We Got Hooked on Hormonal Birth Control
Holly Grigg-Spall
Has contraception liberated or oppressed women?
Sweetening the Pill breaks the silence on the dark side of hormonal
contraception.
Paperback: 978-1-78099-607-3 ebook: 978-1-78099-608-0

Why Are We the Good Guys?
Reclaiming Your Mind from the Delusions of Propaganda
David Cromwell
A provocative challenge to the standard ideology that Western
power is a benevolent force in the world.
Paperback: 978-1-78099-365-2 ebook: 978-1-78099-366-9

The Writing on the Wall
On the Decomposition of Capitalism and its Critics
Anselm Jappe, Alastair Hemmens
A new approach to the meaning of social emancipation.
Paperback: 978-1-78535-581-3 ebook: 978-1-78535-582-0

Neglected or Misunderstood
The Radical Feminism of Shulamith Firestone
Victoria Margree
An interrogation of issues surrounding gender, biology,
sexuality, work and technology, and the ways in which our
imaginations continue to be in thrall to ideologies of maternity
and the nuclear family.
Paperback: 978-1-78535-539-4 ebook: 978-1-78535-540-0

How to Dismantle the NHS in 10 Easy Steps (Second Edition)
Youssef El-Gingihy
The story of how your NHS was sold off and why you will have
to buy private health insurance soon. A new expanded second
edition with chapters on junior doctors' strikes and government
blueprints for US-style healthcare.
Paperback: 978-1-78904-178-1 ebook: 978-1-78904-179-8

Digesting Recipes
The Art of Culinary Notation
Susannah Worth
A recipe is an instruction, the imperative tone of the expert, but
this constraint can offer its own kind of potential. A recipe need
not be a domestic trap but might instead offer escape —
something to fantasise about or aspire to.
Paperback: 978-1-78279-860-6 ebook: 978-1-78279-859-0

Most titles are published in paperback and as an ebook.
Paperbacks are available in traditional bookshops. Both print
and ebook formats are available online.
Follow us at:
https://www.facebook.com/ZeroBooks
https://twitter.com/Zer0Books
https://www.instagram.com/zero.books

For video content, author interviews and more, please subscribe to our YouTube channel:

zer0repeater

Follow us on social media for book news, promotions and more:

Facebook: ZeroBooks

Instagram: @zero.books

X: @Zer0Books

Tik Tok: @zer0repeater